BLS WORKING PAPERS

U.S. DEPARTMENT OF LABOR
Bureau of Labor Statistics

OFFICE OF PRICES AND LIVING
CONDITIONS

Some Explanations for Changes in the Distribution of
Household Income in Slovakia: 1988 and 1996

Thesia I. Garner, U.S. Bureau of Labor Statistics
Katherine Terrell, University of Michigan Business School

Working Paper 345
July 2001 (revised December 2001)

The views expressed are those of the authors and do not necessarily reflect the policies of the U.S. Bureau of Labor Statistics or the views of other staff members. Terrell's research was supported by the World Bank.

SOME EXPLANATIONS FOR CHANGES IN
THE DISTRIBUTION OF HOUSEHOLD INCOME
IN SLOVAKIA: 1988 AND 1996

Thesia I. Garner
PSB, Room 3105, 2 Mass. Ave. N.E.
Bureau of Labor Statistics
Washington, D. C. 20212
U.S.A.
Garner_T@BLS.gov
Telephone: (202) 691-6576
Fax: (202) 691-6583

Katherine Terrell
William Davidson Institute and
University of Michigan Business School
Ann Arbor, MI 48109
U.S.A.
terrell@umich.edu
Telephone: (734) 615-4558
Fax: (734) 936-8715

Paper version: December 12, 2001

JEL classifications:
> O5 Income Distribution
> P2 Socialist and Transition Economies
> P3 Socialist Institutions and Their Transitions

An earlier version of this paper was presented at the International Atlantic Economic Conference in Philadelphia, Pennsylvania, in October 2001. We appreciate the comments of Lisa Wilder, our conference paper discussant, and those of others attending the session. We thank the Slovak Statistical Office and CERGE-EI for making the Slovak Microcensus data available to us. Thanks are also extended to Stephan Jurajda, Renata Kosova and Petr Sedlak for research assistance. Terrell's work for this project was supported by The World Bank.

This paper is also available as Working Paper No. 345, Bureau of Labor Statistics, and Working Paper No. 377, and The William Davidson Institute, University of Michigan Business School.

The views expressed are those of the author and do not reflect the policies of the Bureau of Labor Statistics (BLS) or the views of other BLS staff members.

Abstract

This paper measures the change in overall net monetary income inequality during the first seven years of transition and considers the relative importance of two possible explanations for the increase in inequality. These are a) changes in the sources of household income, and b) changes in household composition. Changes in the sources of household income reflect the role of the government and market during the transition period, while changes in household composition reflect social reactions to the changing economic environment. We find that the increase in inequality in labor income drove the large increase in overall inequality (i.e., the Gini index of household per capita income rose from 0.195 in 1988 to 0.263 in 1996). Changes in the distribution of pensions and other social payments mitigated the rise in earnings inequality, with the latter playing a more important role in reducing changes in overall income inequality over time. We show large shifts in the demographic composition of households over this period including far fewer households with children, far more households headed by pensioners, increases in the number of one-person households and decreases in large (five person) households. Although our results suggest that these shifts in the demographic composition of households contribute to increasing overall inequality, by increasing between group inequality, relatively more of the change in inequality over time is accounted for by increases in within group inequality. We conclude that over the first seven years of the transition labor market forces drove changes in overall inequality in Slovakia to a much greater extent than changes in the government's social safety net or in personal decisions about household formation.

1. Introduction

Under the Soviet system, the Central and East European (CEE) countries maintained the most equal distributions of income in the world. Hence greater income inequality was an expected outcome of the transition from a command to a market economy. Indeed, as prices were liberalized and market forces unleashed, workers with scarce skills saw their earnings rise, while others suffered severe declines in their earnings and even unemployment (see e.g., Terrell, 1999 for a description of winners and losers in the emerging labor market of transition economies).

As expected, we find in our earlier study (Garner and Terrell, 1998) that Slovakia experienced a substantial increase in the inequality of labor earnings during the first four years of transition (1989-1993), however the surprizing result was the very small increase in overall income inequality.[1] Using *Family Budget Survey (FBS)* data, we found the Gini coefficient for total household income per capita rose from 0.157 to 0.168 over this period, whereas the Gini for per capita earnings from labor rose from 0.281 to 0.344 (with much of the rise resulting from self-employment income). The increase in total income inequality arising from this earnings component was almost completely mitigated by changes in the incidence of taxes and the distribution of transfers, with the former playing a slightly more important role than the latter.

In this paper we build on our earlier work to learn about the extent to which inequality increased as the transition progressed to 1996 and to examine some potential explanations for the increase in inequality over this period. We compare inequality before the transition began, in 1988, to the level of inequality eight years later using *Microcensus* data. This is a larger database than the *FBS*, which we used earlier, and it is designed to be representative of the total population with its own set of weights.[2] As in our previous work, we decompose changes in total inequality by changes in sources of income (e.g., earnings from labor, transfer income). In this way we examine the extent to which the labor market affected the distribution of income and the role that the government played in providing a social safety net in 1996 compared to 1988 (and to 1993). Moreover, in this paper we explore an additional factor: the extent to which changes in the demographic composition of households may help explain changes in income inequality over these eight years. The transition process that Slovakia has been undertaking since 1989 has impacted both of these channels of income inequality.

2. Transition in Slovakia

The Slovak economy experienced an enormous transformation during the 1988-1996 period. The macroeconomic statistics in Table 1 indicate the tremendous growth of the private sector as its share of GDP rose from about 5 percent in 1990 to 70 percent in 1996. As in all the Central and East European economies, GDP fell for the first four years of transition (by an average of almost 7 percent a year) but rebounded in 1994 with strong growth through 1996, the end of our period of analysis. Inflation rose by 58 percent during the year that the government liberalized all prices (1991), fell to single digits in 1992 and then rose to 25.7 percent in 1993, the year of the "Velvet Divorce" with the Czech Republic. The decline in output impacted the level of employment, which in 1996 was still only 84.5 percent of the level in 1989. This was accompanied by large

---

[1] We refer to after-tax income, including in-kind payments.
[2] For our earlier study, we created population weights using the *Microcensus* and *FBS* data to make the FBS data as representative as possible. The Central Statistical Office does not produce population weights for the *FBS*.

sectoral shifts in the structure of employment away from agriculture and industry (including manufacturing and utilities), which declined by 44.2 percent and 26.8 percent, respectively. Employment in the service sector absorbed some but not all of the outflows as it grew by 12.1. (*Slovak Statistical Yearbook*, 1997.) Hence unemployment rates were fairly high -- ranging from 10 percent to 14 percent -- throughout the period under analysis.

As a result of all these structural changes in the economy, individuals were faced with much uncertainty about both their job security and the purchasing power of their income during this period. This uncertainty had an impact on the family formation and household structure of the Slovakian people. As seen in Table 2, marriage rates and birth rates declined tremendously from 1989 to 1996, while the divorce rate rose only slightly over the time period. Not surprisingly, the rate of natural increase (the rate at which the population grows based on birth and death rates) fell from 5.0 to 1.6 over this period. Unlike the dramatic case of Russia, where the male mortality rate rose during the transition, the death rate and the infant mortality rate fell over the period.

In this paper we examine how this changing environment affected the distribution of income over time. After measuring the change in overall inequality, we consider the relative importance of two possible explanations for the increase in inequality: a) changes in the sources of household income, and b) changes in the household composition. Changes in the sources of household income reflect the role of the government and market during the transition period, while changes in household composition reflect social reactions to the changing environment. We note that these changes affect the distribution of total income by changing both the numbers of people in different demographic groups as well as the distribution of incomes *per se*.

3. Methods and Data

3.1 Data

The data for this analysis are from the *Microcensuses* taken in 1989 and 1997. Data for each survey refer to income in each previous year. The sample for the first survey represents approximately 5 percent of the households who were living in Slovakia in 1988 (a subsample of the one used for the Czechoslovak *Microcensus)*. The unit of sample selection is the house or apartment. Data are available by common budget households, defined as a set of persons in the same dwelling who share the main household expenditures. People living in the dwelling declared their status according to their sharing of expenditures (Atkinson and Micklewright, 1992). The sample for the 1997 *Microcensus* was created by selecting one percent of all households living in Slovakia in 1997 following a similar procedure as was used for the earlier surveys (Slovak Central Statistical Office website 2001). The 1988 data set includes information on 31,600 households and the 1996 data set includes data on 16,336 households.

3.2 Distributional and Inequality Measurement

Our analysis of overall inequality uses deciles, Lorenz curves (L), concentration curves, and inequality indices based on the ranking of population weighted persons by their household adult equivalent total income. The indices include the standard Gini coefficient (G) and three generalized entropy measures: one half the square of the coefficient of variation (CV), the Theil coefficient (T), and the mean logarithmic

5

deviation (D).[3] The Lorenz curve for discrete distributions, in our case deciles, can be defined as (Lambert 1993):

$$L\left(\frac{j}{10}\right) = \sum_{i=1}^{10} \frac{Y_i}{Y} \text{ where } 1 \leq j \leq 10 \text{ and } Y = \sum_{i=1}^{10} Y_i . \tag{1}$$

The concentration curve in our case simply keeps the population deciles ordered according to total income and plots the cumulative shares of one of its components on the vertical axis (see Lambert 1993).[4]

The indices of inequality can be defined as:

$$G = \sum_i \sum_j \frac{|Y_i - Y_j|}{2n^2 \overline{Y}} \tag{2}$$

$$\frac{(CV)^2}{2} = \frac{1}{2n} \sum_{i=1}^{n} \left[\left(\frac{Y_i}{\overline{Y}}\right)^2 - 1\right] \tag{3}$$

$$T = (1/n)\sum_{i=1}^{n} \left(\frac{Y_i}{\overline{Y}}\right) \ln\left(\frac{Y_i}{\overline{Y}}\right) \tag{4}$$

$$D = (1/n)\sum_{i=1}^{n} \ln\left(\frac{\overline{Y}}{Y_i}\right) \tag{5}$$

where Y_i = the rank weighted income, $\overline{Y}$ = the mean income, and n = the number of income units (persons in the population in our case). Each of the overall measures differs in its sensitivity to income variations at different levels of the distribution. For equidistant transfers, the Gini index is considered to be more sensitive to transfers around the

---

[3] For definitions of these measures of inequality see Coulter et al., 1992
[4] Forster and Pillizzari (2000) refer to the concentration curve as the pseudo-Lorenz curve in their report on income distribution and poverty in the OECD area.

mode, while the Theil measure and one-half the square of the coefficient of variation are more sensitive to transfers at the top of the distribution. The mean logarithmic deviation is relatively more responsive to transfers at the lower end of the distribution.

If the values of all the indices are higher in year t than they are in year t-1, then it can be said that the distribution of income is more unequal in year t. When one Lorenz curve lies above another at one or more points, and does not lie below it at any point, then there is clear Lorenz dominance. However, if one Lorenz curve crosses the other, no conclusions can be drawn regarding relative inequality.

Household data from the *Microcensus* are the basis of our analysis. However, since the focus of this research is the inequality of income across individuals, we allocate adjusted household income to each household member. This weighting results in the individual distribution rather than household distribution of income. The amount of adjusted (or "equivalent") income per person in each household unit is calculated by dividing total household income by the number of equivalent adults in the household. We examine the robustness of our results using four different equivalence scales:

- the *OECD used equivalence scale*[5]
  first adult receives a weight of 1, each additional adult receives a weight of 0.7, and each child a weight of 0.5

- the *Luxembourg Income scale* (LIS)
  the square root of household size

- *per capita* (PC) adjustment
  each person receives a weight of one

3.3 Decomposition Analysis

We undertake two types of decompositions in order to understand which factors are important in contributing to the levels of inequality in each year and changes in inequality over time. The first decomposition is by sources of income and the second is by demographic composition of the household.

Total household income is defined as the sum of monetary income net of taxes (wage taxes, other taxes, and fees) plus the cash value of in-kind income.[6] We analyze the following six sources of income for 1988 and 1996:

- **Earned Income**

    1. Earnings from any non-agricultural employment ("wage income")[7]
    2. Earnings from agricultural employment

- **Social Payments**

    3. Pensions
    4. Other social payments which include:[8]
        - *Sickness Related Benefits* (which include income from health insurance and financial support while taking care of a family member);
        - *Unemployment Benefits* (in 1996 only)
        - *Child Allowances*
        - *Social Assistance and Other Family Benefits* (including maternity leave, and parental allowances)

- **Other Income**

    5. In-kind income
    6. Other monetary income, which includes income from property, institutions or private persons and income from abroad.

To analyze the share of inequality due to each of these sources of income, we use the Lerman and Yitzhaki (1985, 1989, 1994) decomposition of the Gini.[9] The Lerman

---

[5] The OECD did not create the scale but it was used in several of its earlier publications.

[6] We were unable to analyze taxes since this was available separately only in 1988.

[7] This includes income from the self-employed. We would have liked to analyze self-employment income separately but this was not possible given the construction of the data set in 1988.

[8] We are unable to separate out the distributional impact of the subgroups of social payments over time since the categories in 1988 are defined differently than they are in 1996.

and Yitzhaki method decomposes the Gini into three terms: the Gini of the factor component (G_g), the correlation of the factor component with the cumulative distribution of overall income (R_g), and the share of the factor component in overall income, (S_g):

$$G = \sum_{g=1}^{G} G_g R_g S_g \qquad (6)$$

where:

$$G_g = \frac{2 \, \text{cov}\left[y^g, F^g \right]}{\overline{y}^g}, \qquad (6a)$$

$$R_g = \frac{\text{cov}\left[y^g F \right]}{\text{cov}\left[y^g, F^g \right]} \qquad (6b)$$

$$S^g = \frac{\overline{y}^g}{\overline{Y}} \qquad (6c)$$

where $y^1 \dots y^g$ represent the income levels of factor components g, F^g represents the cumulative distribution of y^g and $\overline{Y}^g$ represents the mean. F is the cumulative distribution of Y and $\overline{Y}$ is the mean of overall income.

In order to analyze the effect of household demographic composition on income inequality, we decompose two indices that are members of the Generalized Entropy (GE) measures of inequality measures, the Theil and the mean log deviation indices. Both are additively decomposable by population subgroups (Shorrocks, 1984). To define these indices, let the population be partitioned into k mutually exclusive sub-groups, for

---

[9] Lerman (1999) wrote in a recent survey article, "It is now well understood that the seemingly simple question 'what is the role of an income source in overall income inequality' is complex." Surely, part of the difficulty is that "a source's contribution to inequality depends not only on aspects of the source itself but also on how it interacts with other sources." However, this does not invalidate the source decomposition.

example, household composition. The additive decomposability of T and D can be illustrated by re-writing equations (4) and (5) as follows:

$$T = \Sigma_k v_k \lambda_k T_k + \Sigma_k v_k \lambda_k \ln[\lambda_k]$$ (7)

and

$$D = \Sigma_k v_k D_k + \Sigma_k v_k \ln(1/\lambda_k)$$ (8)

where $v_k = n_k / n$ is the proportion of the population in group k, $\lambda_k = \overline{Y}_k / \overline{Y}$ is group k's mean income relative to that of the whole population, and $v_k \lambda_k$ is the income share of group k in overall income. For each index presented in (7) and (8), total inequality can be expressed as the sum of two contributions: the first term being the "within-group" component (the weighted sum of the inequalities within each sub-group) and the second term is the "between group" component (the inequality remaining if each person's income were equal to his/her sub-group's mean income).

We decompose inequality changes and focus on the mean log deviation measure (D) since is provides a useful decompositional formulation.[10] The change in inequality over the two years, t and $t+1$ can be written as

$$\Delta_0 \approx \Sigma_k \overline{v}_k \Delta I_{0k} + \Sigma_k \overline{I}_{0k} \Delta v_k + \Sigma_k \left(\overline{\lambda}_k - \overline{\ln(\lambda_k)} \right) \Delta v_k + \Sigma_k (\overline{\theta}_k - \overline{v}_k) \Delta \ln(\overline{Y}_k))$$ (9)

$$\qquad\quad \text{term A} \qquad\quad \text{term B} \qquad\qquad \text{term C} \qquad\qquad\quad \text{term D}$$

The change operator is Δ, and a bar over a variable represents the arithmetic mean of the base and current period values.[11] The overall change in inequality can be decomposed

---

[10] According to Jenkins (1995).
[11] Mookherjee and Shorrocks (1992) are credited with creating the decomposition. See Jenkins (1995) for a further application.

into four parts: term A represents the impact of 'pure' within-group inequality changes over time; terms B and C represent the effect on overall inequality of changes in the population shares on the 'within group' and 'between group' components, respectively. Term D represents relative changes in the subgroup means with $\theta_k = v_k \lambda_k$.

4.   Findings

The startling finding in this paper is how much income inequality increased over the 1988-1996 period compared to the 1988/9-93 period. Whereas we (Garner and Terrell, 1998) found total household per capita income inequality did not increase appreciably from 1989 to 1993, we now find that over the 1988-1996 period it has grown by a relatively large amount. As indicated in Table 3, the Gini indices rise by at least 33 percent between 1988 and 1996 when the per capita Gini rose by only 7 percent between 1989 and 1993. The other measures of inequality (Theil, half the coefficient of variation squared, and the mean log deviation) essentially double in size between 1988 and 1966.[12] We also note that the 1996 Lorenz curve, plotted in Chart 1, shifts out to the right of the 1988 Lorenz curve at each point. In looking for explanations for this rise in inequality, we begin by examining changes in the sources of income.

4.1 Sources of Income

As noted above, we examine six sources of after-tax income: income from labor (subdivided into agricultural and non-agricultural income), social transfers (subdivided into pensions and other social payments) and other income (in-kind income and other monetary income). We describe in this section the distributions of each of these sources

---

[12] We note that in almost all cases the per capita income measures are higher than are those using the OECD and LIS adult equivalent adjustments.

of income in 1988 and 1996 using various methods. Results are presented in Tables 4 and 5 and Charts 1 through 5.[13] Table 4 contains information on the share of income from each of the six sources across all persons within each decile of the income distribution. For example, 23.5 percent of all income is from non-agricultural sources for persons in the first decile in 1988. (Remember, the assumption is that all persons in a household are allocated the income of the household on a per adult equivalent basis. The ranking is by total income while the shares are person-based shares of non-agricultural income.[14]) Table 5 presents results from the decomposition described in equations (6a) to (6c). Charts 1, 2 and 4 present the Lorenz and concentration curves of each source of income. Finally, Charts 3 and 5 provide information on the percentage of households in each decile that have a positive value for a particular source of income.

Clearly the first place to look for an explanation of the significant increase in total income inequality is in the change in the distribution of **earnings from labor**. A comparison of the top with the bottom half of Chart 1, indicates that the distance between the 1996 and 1988 concentration curves for earned income is greater than the distance between the Lorenz curves for total income. This indicates a greater increase in the share of earned income going to persons in the upper end of the distribution relative to the distributional change in overall income.[15]

Decomposing earned income into two sources -- agricultural and non-agricultural -- and plotting their concentrations curves for both years, we learn that the distribution of **earnings from non-agricultural activity** has become far more concentrated among

_____

[13] The results in this section (in Charts 1-5 and in Tables 4 and 5) are based on person-weighted, adult-equivalent (LIS) incomes.
[14] If someone in the household received the income, a share was allocated to each person therein equally.

12

those in the upper end of the distribution. This is an indication that those at the top are gaining even more relative to their position in 1988. Earnings from agricultural income have become more equally distributed across the income distribution over this time period, although those with higher incomes still have a greater percentage of agricultural income compared to those at the lower end (Chart 2).

The numbers in Table 5 indicate that earned non-agricultural income contributes more to total income inequality than any other source in both years and its contribution rose over time. In fact the rise in its contribution is the largest increase from any source of income. Its relative contribution to the Gini based on total income is 78.2 percent in 1988 and then rises to 101.9 percent in 1996. Values greater than one are possible given that some of the income components contribute to reductions in overall income inequality. Although non-agricultural income is more unequally distributed when compared to total household income, its share of the total is quite small, thus reducing its overall impact on inequality.

We next ask, what factors might be driving the changes in the contributions of non-agricultural and agricultural income to overall household income inequality -- changes in the inequality of the source *per se*, or changes in the shares of the population with the particular income factor (or sub-component)? In examining the relationship between the population and distribution of income, we first focus on households who have the income factor as a source. Again, the deciles are based on the person distribution of total income. As seen in Chart 3, in 1988 the percentage of households with earnings from non-agricultural activity was about the same in all deciles with the exception of the

---

[15] Hence, the relative change in inequality between earned ant total income over time is qualitatively similar using the 1988-1996 the *Microcensus* data and the 1989-1993 *Family Budget Survey* data.

bottom two (approximately 90 percent of the households in each of the top seven deciles) But in 1996 the percentages of households with non-agricultural earnings are not as equal across the deciles. In that year over 90 percent of the households in the top four deciles had non-agricultural income as a part of their household incomes, the proportion fell to 80 percent, 70 percent, and 60 percent for the next three deciles, respectively. A smaller share of households in the second to the sixth deciles had non-agricultural income in 1996 compared with 1988 (Table 4).

The increased contribution to total inequality from non-agricultural income over time (from 0.147 to 0.255) can be examined with respect to the decompositional components of the Gini (see equation 6): the factor income share, Gini correlation, and factor Gini. From 1988 to 1996 we find an increase in each of these: the share of total income from this source increased from 0.622 to 0.678, the correlation rose from 0.652 and 0.821, and factor Gini representing the inequality in the distribution of this source rose from 0.362 to 0.458. The relative magnitude of the Gini correlation is an indication that higher non-agricultural incomes are even more correlated with higher total household incomes in 1996 than they were in 1988.

The decreased contribution of agricultural income to total income inequality (the relative contribution of this income source on overall income inequality was 0.238 in 1988 as compared to 0.016 in 1996) appears to arise largely because the share of total income from agriculture for households fell from 0.094 to 0.013 (Table 5). However, the drop in the Gini correlation also contributed to this fall in influence. As seen in Chart 3, the shares of households with some agricultural income declined from 1988 to 1996. We also see that the shares of total income from agriculture within each decile (both based on person weighting) fell over time (Table 4). The distribution of agricultural income seems to have become slightly more unequal as the factor Gini rose by only 11 percent (as compared to 27 percent for non-agricultural income) as seen in Table 5. Although agricultural income became more unequal over the time period, it became less concentrated across the entire income distribution as seen in the lower half of Chart 2.

The income shortfall created by the decline in the overall share of agricultural earnings and the decline in the share of non-agricultural earnings for the lower half of the distribution was perhaps filled by **pension income.** Pension income became a larger share of total income, rising from 0.124 to 0.180 over the time period (Table 5). As seen in Table 4, this is due to the rising share of pension income in each decile, except for the top and bottom ones. The concentration curves for pension income (Chart 4) indicate that it is becoming slightly more directed away from the lower end of the distribution but marginally more directed beginning with the third decile. The curve above the equal line indicates that pensions were clearly concentrated among those who were poorer in 1988. By 1996, those at the lower end of the distribution were receiving a disproportionate lower share of pension income up until about the 30th percentile. After that point, pensions became a larger share relative to the population ranking based on overall income. For example, in 1996, 80 percent of the population had access to about 85 percent of all pension income. In contrast, in 1988, pension incomes were equally concentrated among the population at the 80 percentile.

There was a decrease in the factor Gini for pension income from 1988 to 1996 from 0.755 to .730 (Table 5). And the overall effect of pension income on total income inequality and the difference over time is small: in 1988 this income source contributed to lowering the overall Gini index by 0.016 and by 0.012 in 1996 (Table 5).

Although **other social payments** have fallen as a share of income, from 0.111 to 0.083 (Table 5), their contribution in reducing overall income inequality has increased. The relative contribution to the overall Gini was a reduction of 0.006 percent in 1988 but 0.061 percent in 1996. Clearly these benefits are being more targeted to the lower end of the distribution by 1996. As seen in Table 4, the share of other social payments as a percent of person weighted household income has fallen in the top eight deciles and risen dramatically (from 11 percent to 31 percent for the lowest decile). For the second decile, the increase was only slight. Similarly for households, Chart 5 indicates the share of households with any other social income payments fell in all categories except the lowest decile, where it rose. As seen in Chart 4, in 1988 the poorest 20 percent of the population received less than its share of other social payments, while the top half of the distribution received more. However the concentration curve in 1988 hovers around the 45-degree line.

Although **other monetary income** is only a small share of total income in both years (0.011 and 0.024), its share for the top two deciles rose considerably in 1996 (see Table 4). Similarly, the share of households with other monetary income fell in all but the top decile where it rose (Chart 5). The 1996 concentration curve reveals that other monetary income is more concentrated in the upper range of the income distribution than such income for 1988 (Chart 4). This source of income is quite eclectic, including earnings from abroad as well as income from property and from other people.

Finally, **in-kind income** became more equally concentrated over the total income population (Chart 4). The shares of this income across the deciles fell from 1988 to 1996 but the shares fell in almost the same way (Table 4). The results in Chart 5 reveal a much lower and similarly distributed percentage of households with in-kind income in 1996 as in 1988, with the exception of the top decile. Those in the top decile were most likely to be recipients of in-kind income in 1996.

In summary: overall inequality rose during the period, largely due to changes in non-agricultural earned income and partially due to changes in other monetary income (which includes foreign income). The rise in the contribution of non-agricultural earnings to total income inequality is likely due to not only an increase in this source's inequality but also its other characteristics, it share and correlation with total income..

4.2 Demographic Characteristics of Households

Among other channels, changes in income inequality can be driven by changes in the composition of the household. The demographic shifts we noted in Table 2, regarding the noticeable decline in the marriage rates and live-births are reflected in the structures of the households in the 1988 and 1996 *Microcensus* data. For example, we show in Table 6 that the share of the households with one or more children fell to 33 percent in 1996 from 45 percent in 1988. Similarly, we noted above that the death rates declined slightly, yielding higher life expectancy. We find in the *Microcensus* data that the average age of the head of the household rose as the share of households with heads over 70 years of age increased and the share with heads less than 39 years of age fell.

As a result of the tremendous structural changes in the Slovak economy , with labor being reallocated from the inefficient old state sector to the new private sectors, many people became unemployed or took early retirement. Hence, it is not surprising to note in Table 6 that the head of the household in 1996 is much less likely to be working and more likely to be a pensioner or unemployed compared to 1988. However, the rise in the share of households headed by pensioners – from 26 percent to 35 percent – could also reflect other factors, such as general aging of the population or a change in household formation, in addition to the increase in the number of pensioners brought about by the restructuring. The figures in Table 7 reveal that the number of pensioners rose by about 10 percent from 1989 to 1995 and that the rise was higher among old-age and disability pensioners (14 percent) than among widows (8 percent). As seen in Table 7, the government has maintained the value of pension income by allowing it to rise at the same rate that wages are rising. Hence pensions have been consistently around 45 percent of the average wage over this period. Given these statistics, it is likely that the government's decision to maintain the purchasing power of pensioners at a relatively high level has enabled pensioners to live independently. Consistent with this hypothesis is the finding in Table 6 that there is a decrease in the share of households with five or more persons and an increase in the share with one person.

How do these changes in household composition impact the distribution of income during the 1988 and 1996 periods? We begin to examine this issue by describing the demographic characteristics of the households in each decile in Chart 6. For example, the number of persons per household declined over the period in all but the lowest decile, which in 1996 has more members (2.5) than in 1988 (1.6). This is most likely due to a decline in the number of children per household in each decile, except for the lowest where it rose. Households in the lowest decile are comprised partially of more children, more economically active adults and more unemployed adults (not shown in Chart 6). However, households in the first decile are not composed of more pensioners, The lower right hand chart in Chart 6 indicates that the percentage of households in the first decile with a pensioner head decreased in 1996, while the percentage increased in all other deciles in 1996 relative to 1988.

In order to increase our understanding of the role of demographic characteristics on income inequality, we first decompose overall inequality into the portion due to inequality within each demographic group and the portion arising from the inequality that remained if each person's income was equal to her/his sub-group's mean income (i.e., between group inequality). Following this results, we present the results from the inequality decomposition which reflects changes over time.

The findings from the within demographic decompositions, described in equations (9) and (10), are presented in Table 8. The decompositions are carried out for the six groups previously described in Table 6 plus two new demographic classifications of households based on a combination of the other characteristics.

Not surprisingly, the decompositions for the Theil and mean log deviation indices show that the majority of overall inequality can be explained by inequality from within the groups -- very little is driven by between group differences.[16] Moreover, the increase in inequality over time is being driven by changes in within group inequality since in most cases (six out of eight categories) the between group inequality has fallen over time. For example, in the third category, number of economically active members, the inequality within the groups (i.e., none, one, two, three+ members) represented 56

---

[16] This is the finding in almost all decompositions of this sort – within group inequality is more important than between group inequality in explaining overall inequality.

percent of total inequality in 1988 (i.e., 0.0337/0.0600) and it rose to explain 83 percent of inequality in 1996. The difference in the within group inequality over time was 1.14 of the difference in the overall inequality over time. Hence the share explained by between group inequality was –0.14 of the difference in overall inequality.

The three categories for which the between group inequality is relatively more important are the third (mentioned above), seventh (age of adults with number of adults and number of children) and eighth (if children present and number of economically active members) categories in Table 8. Here the differences in the means (not shown) of each group are relatively larger in explaining overall inequality than the dispersion of income within each group, as compared to the other five categories. Nevertheless, the pattern of greater increase in within group inequality than between group over time still holds.

The analysis of the impact on income inequality of demographic changes in the populations over the 1988 to 1996 period are presented in Table 9. The decomposition in Table 9 yields information on the impact that changes in the following four factors have on changes in overall inequality over time: i) changes in within group inequality (Term A); ii) changes in population shares on the within group component of inequality (Term B); iii) changes in population shares on the between group component of inequality (Term C); and iv) changes in the subgroup mean (Term D). The values in Table 9 are expressed as proportions (or shares) of the total difference in overall inequality. As was learned from the analysis in Table 8, the vast majority of the change in overall inequality in 1988 compared to 1996 was brought about the changes in inequality within each sub-group (e.g., the households with no, one, two or three plus

20

children). In all but two groups -- number of children and economic activity of head of household -- the within group inequality (Term A) grew by more than 100 percent of the change in overall inequality. In all but one group (number of children) the change in the relative subgroup means (Term D) actually lowered the change in overall inequality. Hence, the dispersion within each group grew, but the differences in the relative means of these subgroups fell.

What about the shift in population shares (Terms B and C)? In general they increase inequality but their impact is small compared to the impact of Terms A and D. Moreover, they tend to impact between-group inequality more than within-group inequality. For example, the shift in the population shares of households headed by economically active individuals, pensioners and "other " (e.g., unemployed) increased between group inequality by a larger amount than it impacted within group inequality. Similarly, shifts in the share of the population across categories of "age of pensioner head" increased between group inequality but lowered within group inequality. In sum shifts in the demographic composition of the households are increasing overall inequality over time.

5. Conclusions

We have found a large increase in total income inequality in Slovakia eight years after the beginning of transition. The Gini index of household per capita income (net monetary income plus in-kind income) rose from 0.195 in 1988 to 0.263 in 1996. Using the LIS equivalent household income, the Gini rose from 0.188 to 0.250. In this paper we examine the impact of markets and countervailing government safety nets on this change in inequality over time by analyzing shifts in sources of income, in their distributions, means, shares, and in the percentage of persons with these incomes (based on person allocations). We learned that the earned non-agricultural income contributes most to overall income inequality in each year, due to its large income share and to how unequally it is distributed (Factor Gini). Moreover, in 1996 it accounted for much more of total inequality than it did in 1988 and hence is the single most important factor contributing to the large increase in overall income inequality between 1988 and 1996. The distribution of pension income mitigated overall inequality in both years, but less so in 1996, whereas the distribution of other social payments played a much larger role in reducing income inequality in 1996 than in 1988.

We show there are large shifts in the demographic composition of households over time: far fewer households with children, far more households headed by pensioners, increases in the number of one-person households and decreases in large (five person) households. We find that these shifts in the demographic composition of households are increasing overall inequality, by increasing between group inequality. Their impact is larger than that found for the U.K. by Jenkins (1995) and Mookherjee and Shorrocks (1982). Nevertheless, most of the change in inequality over time is accounted for by increase in within group inequality. And given our finding above, we are lead to believe that this is due to an increase in the dispersion of labor earnings over this period. Finally it is interesting to note that although dispersion of income within each group has grown significantly over time, the differences in the means of each group have actually decreased over time. Hence between group inequality has declined from 1988 to 1996. We conclude that over the first seven years of the transition labor market forces are driving changes in overall inequality in Slovakia to a much greater extent than changes in

the Government's social safety net or in individual's decisions about household formation.

REFERENCES

Atkinson, Anthony B. and John Micklewright (1992), *Economic Transformation in Eastern Europe and the Distribution of Income*, Cambridge University Press.

Buhmann, Brigitte, Lee Rainwater, Guenther Schmaus, and Timothy M. Smeeding (1992), "Equivalence Scales, Well-Being, Inequality, and Poverty: Sensitivity Estimates Across Ten Countries Using the Luxembourg Income Study (LIS) Database," *Review of Income and Wealth*, Vol. 34., No. 2, June: 115-142.

Chase, Robert (1998), "Baby Boom or Bust? Changing Fertility in Post-Communist Czech Republic and Slovakia" William Davidson Institute Working Paper No. 157

Commission of the European Communities (CEC, 1992), *Employment Observatory, Central and Eastern Europe, Employment Trends and Developments*, No. 1, January.

Forster, Michael F. and Michele Pellizzari (2000), *Trends and Driving Factors in Income Distribution and Poverty in the OECD Area*, Labour Market and Social Policy-Occasional Papers No. 42, Directorate for Education, Employment, Labour and Social Affairs, OECD, Paris, France.

Garner, Thesia I. and Katherine Terrell (1998), "A Gini Decompositon Analysis of Inequality in the Czech and Slovak Republics During the Transition," *The Economics of Transition*, 6(1): 23-46.

Jenkins, Stephen P. (1991), "The Measurement of Income Inequality" in Lars Osberg (ed.) *Economic Inequality and Poverty: International Perspectives*. Sharp Publishers: London: 3-38.

Jenkins, Stephen P. (1995), "Accounting for Inequality Trends: Decomposition Analyses for the U.K., 1971-86," *Economica*. 62(245): pp. 29-63.

Lambert, Peter J. (1993), The Distribution and Redistribution of Income, A Mathematical Analysis, Manchester, UK: Manchester University Press.

Lerman R. (1999), "How income sources affect income inequality?" in J.Silber (ed), *Handbook on Income Inequality Measurement*, Dordrecht: Kluwer Academic Publishers.

Lerman, Robert I. and Shlomo Yitzhaki (1985), "Income Inequality Effects by Income Sources: A New Approach and Applications to the U.S.," *Review of Economics and Statistics*, February, Vol. 67: 151-156.

Lerman, Robert I. and Shlomo Yitzhaki (1989), "Improving the Accuracy of Estimates of Gini Coefficients," *Journal of Econometrics*, September, Vol. 42: 43-47.

Lerman, Robert I. and Shlomo Yitzhaki (1994), "The Effect of Marginal Changes in Income Sources on U. S. Income Inequality," *Public Finance Quarterly*, October.

Milanovic, Branko (1992), "Income Distribution in Late Socialism: Poland, Hungary, Czechoslovakia, Yugoslavia, and Bulgaria Compared," Socialist Economies Reform Unit, Country Economics Department, World Bank, Research paper series, paper number 1, March.

Milanovic, Branko (June 1992), "Distributional Impact of Cash and In-Kind Transfers in Eastern Europe and Czechoslovakia," Socialist Economies Reform Unit, Country Economics Department, World Bank, Research paper series, paper number 9.

Mookherjee, D. and A. F. Shorrocks (1982), "A decomposition analysis of the trend in UK income inequality," *Economic Journal*, 92, 886-992.

Podder, Nripesh (1993), "The Disaggregation of the Gini Coefficient by Factor Components and its Applications to Australia," *Review of Income and Wealth*, Series 39, No. 1, March: 51-61

Shorrocks, A. F. (1984), "Inequality Decomposition by Population Subgroups," *Econometrica*, Vol. 52, No. 6: 1369-1385.

Shorrocks, A. F. (1980), "The Class of Additively Decomposable Inequality Measures," *Econometrica*, Vol. 48, No. 3: 613-625.

Slovak Central Statistical Office (2001), website: http://www.statistics.sk/.

Smeeding, Timothy M. (1991), "Cross-National Comparisons of Inequality and Poverty Position," in Lars Osberg (ed.), *Economic Inequality and Poverty: International Perspectives*, New York: M. E. Sharpe, Inc., pp. 39-59.

Tsakloglou P. (1993) "Aspects of inequality in Greece: Measurement, decomposition and inter-temporal change: 1974, 1982," *Journal of Development Economics,* 40: 53-74.

Yitzhaki, Shlomo (1989), "Ginjack and Ginjackw," Fortran program, September 27.

Table 1
Macroeconomic Data for Slovakia

	1990	1991	1992	1993	1994	1995	1996	1997	1998	1999	Source
Economic Growth											
%GDP growth (real)	-2.5	-14.6	-6.5	-3.7	4.9	6.7	6.2	6.2	4.1	1.9	EBRD, EIU
GDP per capita ($US)	2,710	2,052	2,213	2,258	2,571	3,240	3,495	3,679	3,802	3,970	EBRD, OECD
Prices											
CPI Index (% change)	18.4	58.3	9.1	25.1	11.7	7.2	5.4	6.4	5.6	14.0	World Bank, EBRD, DataStream
Trade											
Current Account Balance (%GDP)	-6.1	3	1.6	-5	4.8	2.3	-11.2	-10	-10.1	-5.5	World Bank, EBRD, EIU
Market Liberlization											
Private Sector Share of GDP (%)	5	NA	NA	NA	55	60	70	75	75	75	World Bank, EBRD
Labor Markets											
Unemployment Rate (%)	1.5	11.8	10.3	12.2	13.7	13.1	11.1	11.6	11.9	19.2	EBRD, Business Central Europe
% change in productivity	NA	NA	NA	NA	6.8	4.0	2.5	4.1	11.5	2.0	EBRD
% change in wages	NA	NA	NA	NA	7.0	5.7	9.8	7.5	6.1	-3.9	EBRD
Index of Employment Levels (1989=1)*	0.982	0.859	0.868	0.846	0.837	0.857	0.845	0.826	0.818	0.780	UNDP

*Employment in 1989 was 2,504,079

Table 2

Slovakia: Population Changes in Rates per 1,000 Inhabitants

Indicator	1989	1990	1991	1992	1993	1994	1995	1996
Marriages	6.90	7.60	6.20	6.40	5.80	5.30	5.10	5.10
Divorces	1.57	1.67	1.49	1.52	1.53	1.62	1.67	1.75
Live-Births	15.20	15.10	14.90	14.10	13.80	12.40	11.40	11.20
Deaths	10.20	10.30	10.30	10.10	9.90	9.60	9.80	9.50
Infant Mortality	13.50	12.00	13.20	12.60	10.60	11.20	11.00	11.00
Natural Increase	5.00	4.80	4.60	4.00	3.90	2.80	1.60	1.70

Source: *Statistical Yearbook of the Slovak Republic, 1996* (p. 154)

Table 3

Slovakia: Overall Income Inequality: 1988 and 1996[1]

	1988 (n=31,606)			1996 (n=16,336)			% difference (1996 vs. 1988)		
	OECD	LIS	PC	OECD	LIS	PC	OECD	LIS	PC
Log Deviation	0.050	0.062	0.062	0.125	0.128	0.142	150.1	107.2	129.3
Thiel	0.051	0.060	0.065	0.111	0.112	0.128	117.6	86.7	96.9
(CV)²/2	0.060	0.067	0.079	0.134	0.131	0.157	123.8	96.1	99.2
Gini	0.172	0.188	0.195	0.243	0.25	0.263	41.3	33.7	34.9

Data: Slovak Republic *Microcensus* 1988 and 1996

[1]Household equivalent after tax monetary plus in-kind income, LIS equivalence scale; person weighted distribution

Table 4
Slovakia: Income Distribution[1] by Source within Each Decile

1988

Decile	Earned Income		Social Payments		Other monetary income	In-Kind Income	Total
	Non-Agricultural	Agricultural	Pension	Excluding pension			
1	23.5%	1.7%	58.1%	11.3%	2.1%	3.4%	100.0%
2	48.6%	3.6%	24.6%	18.3%	1.8%	3.1%	100.0%
3	59.1%	4.6%	14.1%	18.0%	1.3%	2.7%	100.0%
4	65.6%	4.8%	10.0%	16.1%	0.8%	2.6%	100.0%
5	68.0%	6.0%	8.3%	14.0%	0.9%	2.8%	100.0%
6	68.0%	7.5%	8.1%	12.1%	0.8%	3.4%	100.0%
7	67.1%	9.3%	8.6%	10.3%	0.9%	3.7%	100.0%
8	66.9%	10.3%	9.0%	8.5%	0.9%	4.4%	100.0%
9	66.2%	12.2%	8.7%	7.2%	1.0%	4.6%	100.0%
10	61.5%	18.8%	7.6%	5.4%	1.4%	5.3%	100.0%

[1]Decile ranking based on household adult equivalent after tax monetary plus in-kind income with source income also equalized.
Both based on LIS equivalence scale (square root of family size). Person weighted distribution.

Decile	Earned Income		Social Payments		Other monetary income	In-Kind Income	Total
	Non-Agricultural	Agricultural	Pension	Excluding pension			
1	32.7%	0.7%	30.9%	31.4%	1.5%	2.9%	100.0%
2	39.8%	0.9%	36.2%	20.1%	1.3%	1.7%	100.0%
3	46.7%	1.1%	33.2%	16.1%	1.0%	1.9%	100.0%
4	50.8%	1.2%	32.2%	12.5%	1.2%	2.0%	100.0%
5	57.9%	0.8%	26.9%	11.1%	0.9%	2.4%	100.0%
6	65.6%	1.8%	20.1%	8.7%	1.2%	2.6%	100.0%
7	73.4%	1.5%	14.6%	6.9%	1.2%	2.3%	100.0%
8	76.8%	1.5%	12.5%	5.0%	1.6%	2.6%	100.0%
9	77.9%	1.8%	11.5%	3.6%	2.5%	2.6%	100.0%
10	85.5%	1.1%	4.5%	1.5%	6.0%	1.4%	100.0%

[1]Decile ranking based on household adult equivalent after tax monetary plus in-kind income with source income also equalized.
Both based on LIS equivalence scale (square root of family size). Person weighted distribution.

Table 5
Slovakia: Decomposition by Source of Income

	Share of Total Income	Gini Correlation	Factor Gini	Contribution to Overall Gini	Relative Contribution to Gini
1988					
earned non-agricultural income	0.622	0.652	0.362	0.147	0.782
earned agricultural income	0.094	0.537	0.881	0.045	0.238
pension income	0.124	-0.172	0.755	-0.016	-0.085
other social payments	0.111	-0.020	0.474	-0.001	-0.006
other monetary incomes	0.011	0.145	0.927	0.002	0.008
in-kind income	0.038	0.426	0.721	0.012	0.063
TOTAL				**0.188**	**1.000**
1996					
earned non-agricultural income	0.678	0.821	0.458	0.255	1.019
earned agricultural income	0.013	0.312	0.979	0.004	0.016
pension income	0.180	-0.093	0.730	-0.012	-0.049
other social payments	0.083	-0.281	0.653	-0.015	-0.061
other monetary incomes	0.024	0.598	0.972	0.014	0.056
in-kind income	0.022	0.262	0.853	0.005	0.020
TOTAL				**0.250**	**1.000**

[1]Decile ranking based on household adult equivalent after tax monetary plus in-kind income with source income also equivalized.
Both based on LIS equivalence scale (square root of family size). Person weighted distribution.

N.B.: Household LIS equivalent after tax monetary income, including in-kind, in current CSK crowns for 1988 and SR crowns for 1996, based on person weights, whose mean is 39410 in 1988 and 76566 in 1996.

Table 6
Slovakia: Demographic Composition of the Household (Percentage Distribution of Households)

Charactersitic	1988	1996	Charactersitic	1988	1996
Children Present in Household			**Age of Head**		
no children	55.4	67.0	head <=29 years of age	10.1	5.9
children present	44.6	33.0	head 30-34 years of age	11.9	7.0
Number of Children			head 35-39 years of age	12.5	9.4
no children	55.4	67.0	head 40-44 years of age	10.6	13.0
one child	16.8	16.4	head 45-49 years of age	9.2	13.4
two children	19.7	12.9	head 50-54 years of age	8.6	10.3
three or more children	8.1	3.7	head 55-59 years of age	9.2	8.7
Economic Activity of Head			head 60-64 years of age	8.6	8.3
economically active	73.3	60.4	head 65-69 years of age	8.0	8.1
unemployed	none	3.5	head 70+ years of age	11.3	14.8
pensioner	26.4	34.7	missing		1.1
other	0.3	1.4	**Age of Pensioner Head**		
Household Size			no pensioners	72.7	65.3
one person	17.8	21.2	pensioner head <= 59 years of age	4.4	5.2
two persons	24.3	23.0	pensioner head 60-64 years of age	5.9	6.9
three persons	17.6	17.7	pensioner head 65-69 years of age	6.7	7.9
four persons	24.1	25.4	pensioner head 70+years of age	10.3	14.8
five persons	10.9	8.7	**No. of Econ. Active Members**		
six or more persons	5.3	4.0	no econ active members	21.5	28.2
			one econ active member	25.0	26.6
			two econ active members	42.0	33.9
			3 or more econ active members	11.5	11.3

Table7
Slovakia: Number of Pensioners and Average Monthly Pension,[1] 1989-1995

Number of Pensioners (in thousands)

	1989	1990	1991	1992	1993	1994	1995
Total	1065	1087	1124	1156	1172	1178	1173
Old-Age	488	506	532	548	553	556	558
Disability[2**]	218	223	230	243	252	256	248
Widow	270	275	279	283	286	288	291

Average Monthly Pension (in Slovak crowns)

	1989	1990	1991	1992	1993	1994	1995
Old-Age	1432	1550	1884	2058	2367	2852	3102
Disability[2]	1310	1413	1750	1940	2247	2714	2950
Widow	742	825	1007	1118	1255	1431	1594

Average Pension as a Share of the Wage

	1989	1990	1991	1992	1993	1994	1995
Old-Age	46.3%	48.2%	50.3%	45.5%	45.0%	46.8%	43.8%
Disability[2]	42.4%	43.9%	46.7%	42.9%	42.7%	44.6%	41.7%
Widow	24.0%	25.6%	26.9%	24.7%	23.9%	23.5%	22.5%

Source: *Statistical Yearbook of the Slovak Republic*, 1994 (p.148, 406) and 1996 (p.180, 476)

[1] Monthly level of pension paid out excluding child support bonus and disability benefits

[2] For the handicapped

Table 8
Within-Group and Between-Group Income Inequality[1] in Slovakia: 1988 and 1996

Category Sample		Year	Theil			Mean Log Deviation		
			Aggregate Inequality	Within-group inequality	Between-group inequality	Aggregate Inequality	Within-group inequality	Between-group inequality
1	Number of Children	1988	0.0600	0.0585	0.0015	0.0618	0.0603	0.0015
		1996	0.1124	0.1090	0.0034	0.1284	0.1248	0.0036
2	Household Size	1988	0.0600	0.0522	0.0077	0.0618	0.0529	0.0089
		1996	0.1124	0.1091	0.0032	0.1284	0.1250	0.0034
3	No. of Econ. Active Members	1988	0.0600	0.0337	0.0263	0.0618	0.0337	0.0281
		1996	0.1124	0.0935	0.0189	0.1284	0.1089	0.0195
4	Economic Activity of Head	1988	0.0600	0.0525	0.0075	0.0618	0.0536	0.0082
		1996	0.1124	0.1039	0.0085	0.1284	0.1192	0.0092
5	Age of Head	1988	0.0600	0.0502	0.0098	0.0618	0.0517	0.0101
		1996	0.1124	0.1071	0.0052	0.1284	0.1230	0.0054
6	Age of Pensioner Head	1988	0.0600	0.0529	0.0071	0.0618	0.0537	0.0081
		1996	0.1124	0.1088	0.0035	0.1284	0.1247	0.0037
7	Age of Adults, No. of Adults and No. of Children	1988	0.0600	0.0413	0.0187	0.0618	0.0415	0.0203
		1996	0.1124	0.0995	0.0129	0.1284	0.1146	0.0138
8	Children and Econ. Active Members	1988	0.0600	0.0299	0.0301	0.0618	0.0299	0.0318
		1996	0.1124	0.0878	0.0245	0.1284	0.1027	0.0257

[1]Decile ranking based on household adult equivalent after tax monetary plus in-kind income with source income also equivalized.
Both based on LIS equivalence scale (square root of family size). Person weighted distribution.

Subgroup defined as follows:

Number of Children: no children, 1 child, two children, 3+ children
Number of HH Members: one, two three, four, five+
Number of economically active members: none, one, two, three+
Economic Activity of Head: economically active, pensioner, other
Age of Head: 15-39, 40-54, 55-64, 65+

Age l.t. 65, no children,two adults; 3) Age l.t. 65, no children, three+ adults; 4) Age l.t. 65, children, two adults; 5) Age l.t. 65, on child, two adults; 6) Age l.t. 65, two children, two adults; 7) Age l.t. 65, three+ children, two adults; 8) Age l.t. 65, children, three+ adults; 9) Age g.t. 65, with and without children, one adult 10) Age g.t. 65, three+ children, no econ active adult; 2) no children, one econ active adult; 3) no children, two econ active adults; 4) no children, three+ econ active adults; 5) children, no econ active adult; 6) children,

Econ. Activity and no. of children: 1) no children, no econ active adult; 2) no children, one econ active adult; 3) no children, two econ active adults; 4) no children, three+ econ active adults; 5) children, no econ active adult; 6) children, one econ active adult; 3) no children, two econ active adults; 4) no children, three+ econ active adults; 5) children, no econ active adult; 6) children,

Age of pensioner: no pensioner head, pensioner l.t. 65, pensioner g.t. eq. 65 years.

one econ active adult; 7) children, two econ active adults; 8) children, three+ econ active adults.

Table 9
Sub-group Decompositions of Changes in Aggregate Income
Inequality: 1988 - 1996[1]

| | Contribution to change in overall inequality due to changes in: | | | |
| | Within Group inequality (Term A) | Population Shares effect on | | Group Mean Incomes (Term D) |
		within (Term B)	between (Term C)	
No. Children	0.889	0.087	-0.022	0.046
Household Size	1.067	0.013	0.015	-0.095
No. Econ. Active Members	1.127	-0.007	0.099	-0.218
Econ. Activity of Head	0.928	0.046	0.128	-0.102
Age of Pensioner Head	1.061	-0.009	0.047	-0.100
No. Children, No. and Age of Adults	1.089	0.009	0.026	-0.125
Children-Econ Active Members	1.077	0.005	0.139	-0.221

[1]Household equivalent after tax monetary plus in-kind income, LIS equivalence scale; person weighted distr bution; Based on the Mean Log Deviation Measure of Inequality.

Subgroup defined as follows:

Number of Children: no children, 1 child, two children, 3+ children

Number of HH Members: one, two three, four, five+

Number of economically active members: none, one, two, three+

Economic Activity of Head: economically active, pensioner, other

Age of Head: 15-39, 40-54, 55-64, 65+

Age of pensioner: no pensioner head, pensioner l.t. 65, pensioner g.t. eq. 65 years.

Age and No. of adults and no. of children: 1) Age l.t. 65, no children,one adult; 2) Age l.t. 65, no children,two adults; 3) Age l.t. 65, no children, three+ adults; 4) Age l.t. 65, children, two adults; 5) Age l.t. 65, on child, two adults; 6) Age I

Econ. Activity and no. of children: 1) no children, no econ active adult; 2) no children, one econ active adult; 3) no children, two econ active adults; 4) no children, three+ econ active adults; 5) children, no econ active adult; 6) children, one

Chart 1
Lorenz Curve and Concentration Curve for All Income

Lorenz Curve: Total Household Income Including In-kind

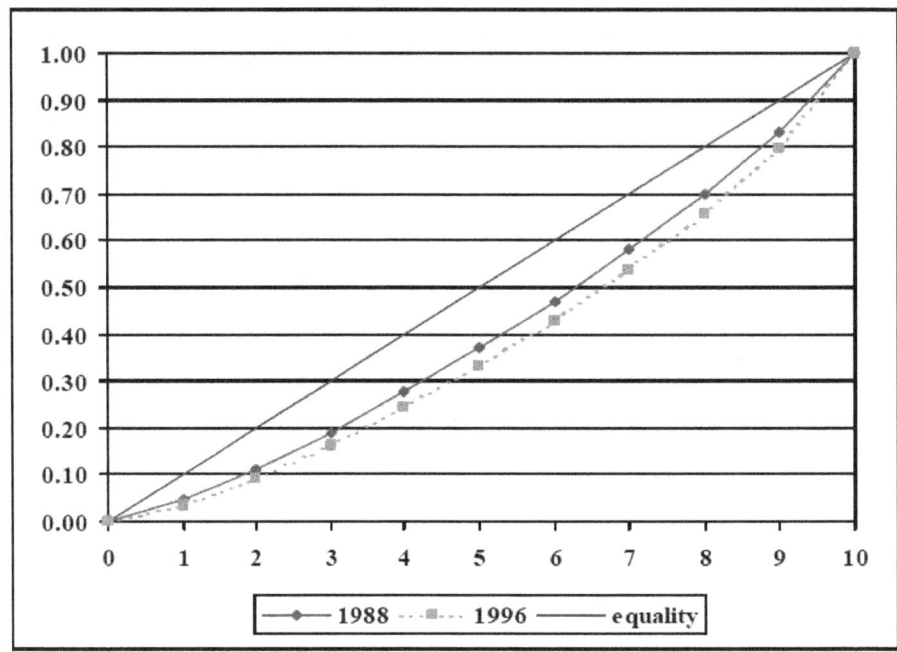

shares of total after tax household income including in-kind

Deciles of persons ranked by equivalent total after tax household income including in-kind -LIS scale

Concentration Curve: All Earned Income

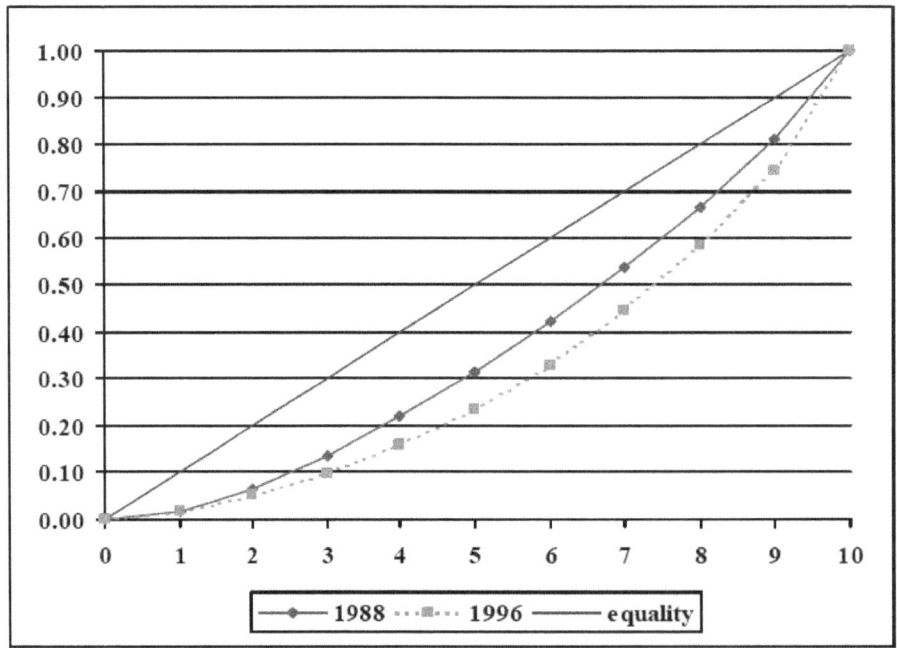

shares of income from working (earned)

Deciles of persons ranked by equivalent total after tax household income including in-kind -LIS scale

Chart 2
Concentration Curves: Non Agricultural vs. Agricultural Income

Non-Agricultural Earned Income

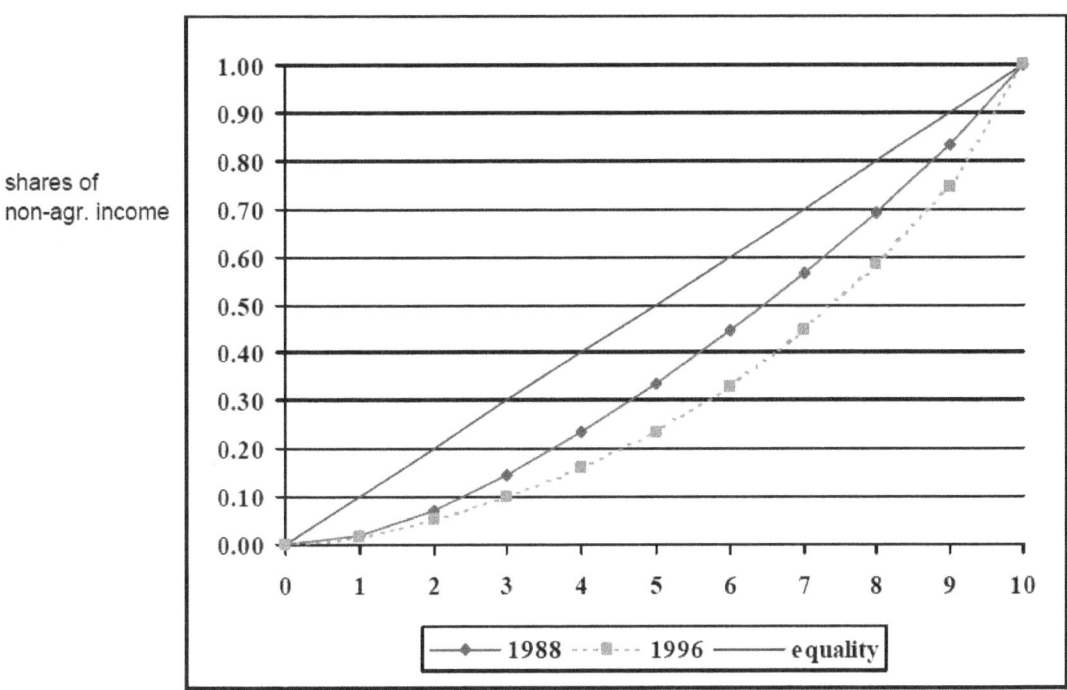

Deciles of persons ranked by equivalent total after tax household income including in-kind -LIS scale

Earned Agricultural Income

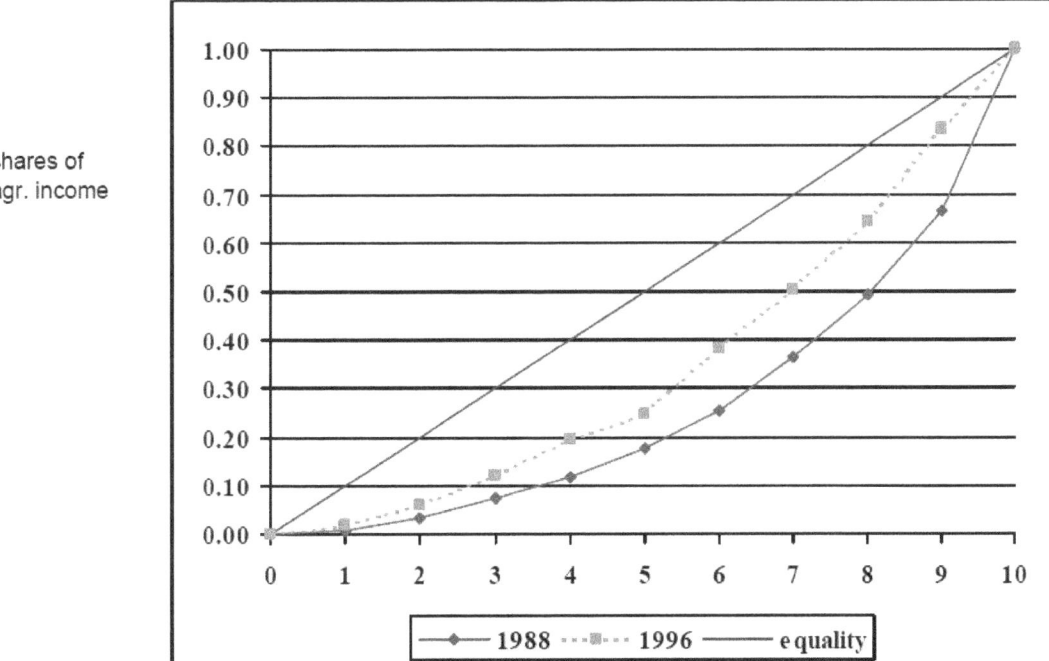

Chart 3

Percentage of Households with Earned Income: Agricultural vs. Non-Agricultural

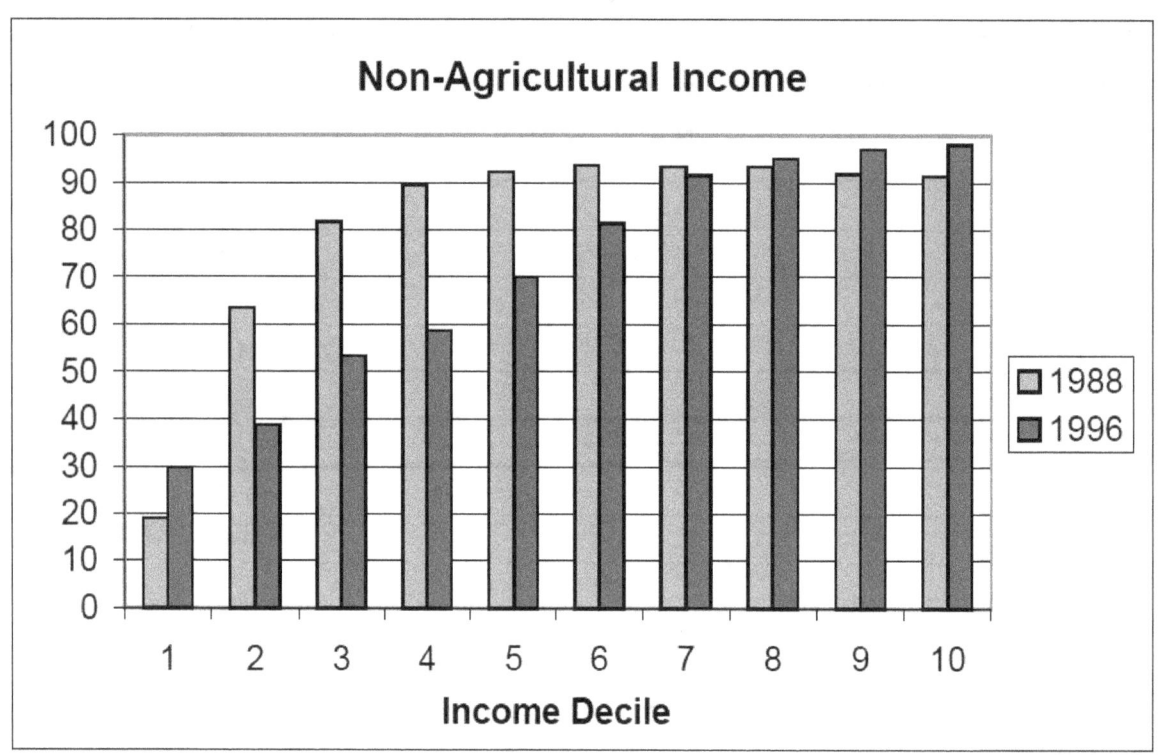

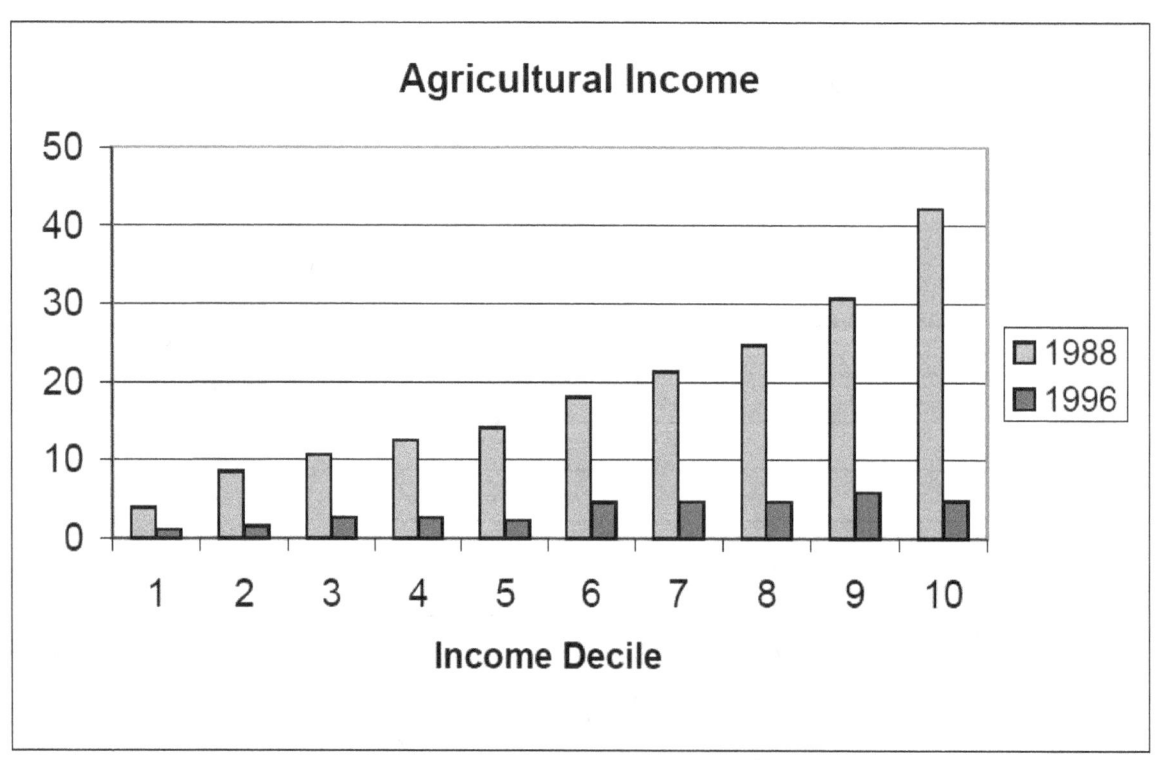

Chart 4
Concentration Curves of Other Source of Income

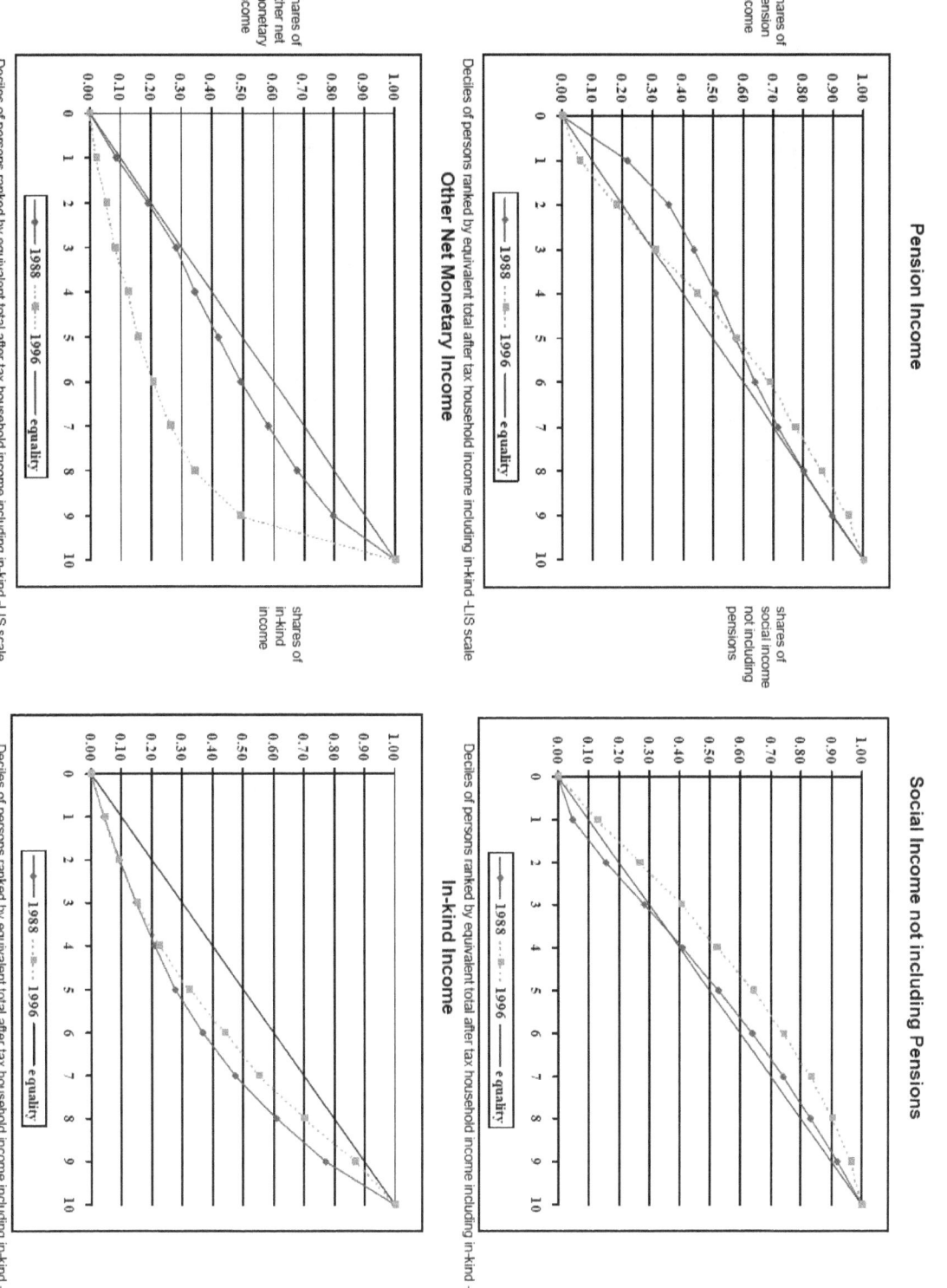

Pension Income

Social Income not including Pensions

Other Net Monetary Income

In-Kind Income

Chart 5

Percentage of Households with Unearned Income by Source

Pension Income

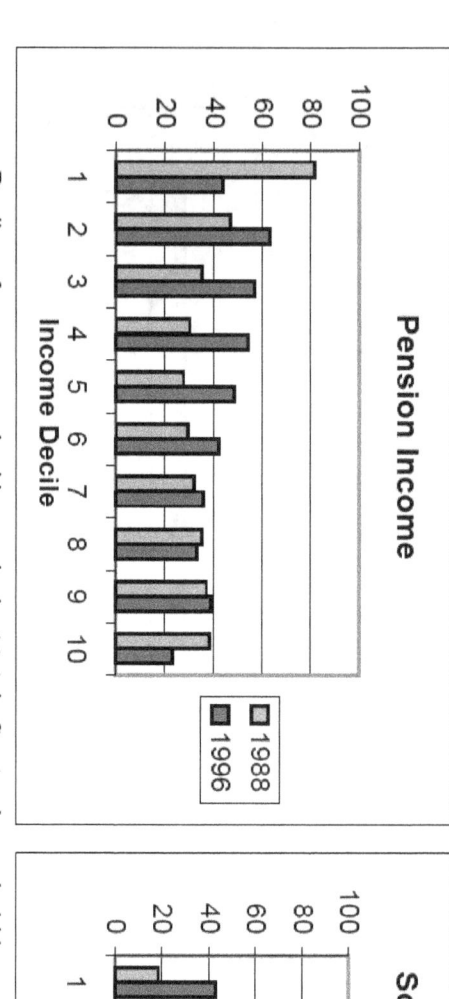

Deciles of persons ranked by equivalent total after tax household income including in-kind -LIS scale

Social Income (excluding pensions)

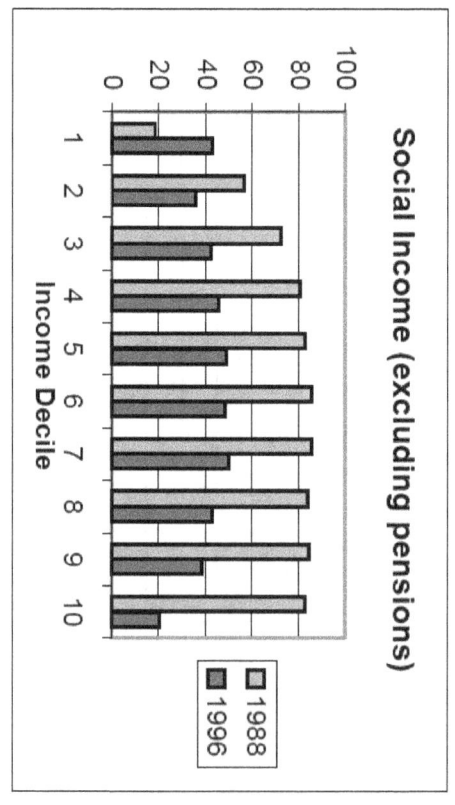

Other Net Monetary Income

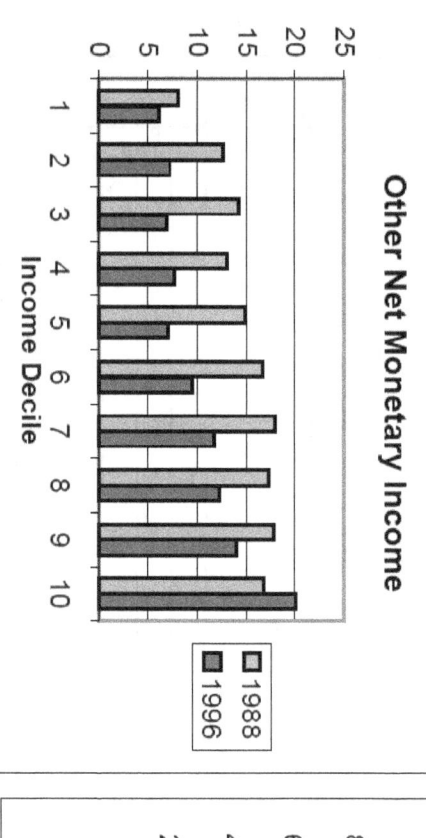

Deciles of persons ranked by equivalent total after tax household income including in-kind -LIS scale

In-Kind Income

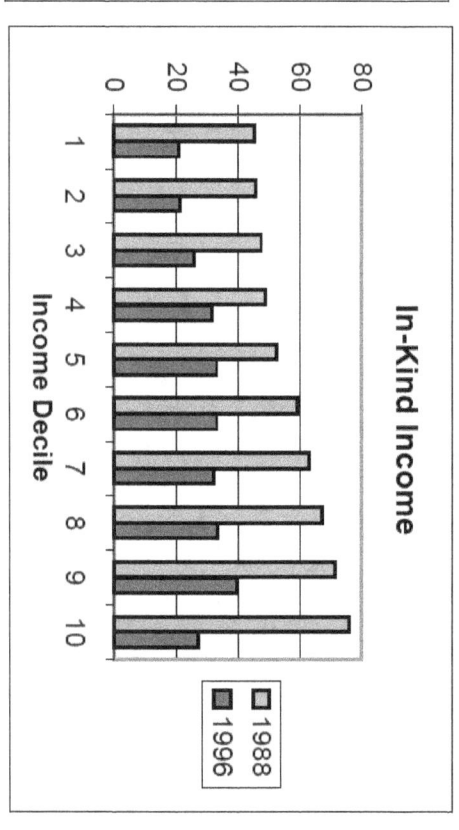

Chart 6
Demographic Characteristics by Income Decile

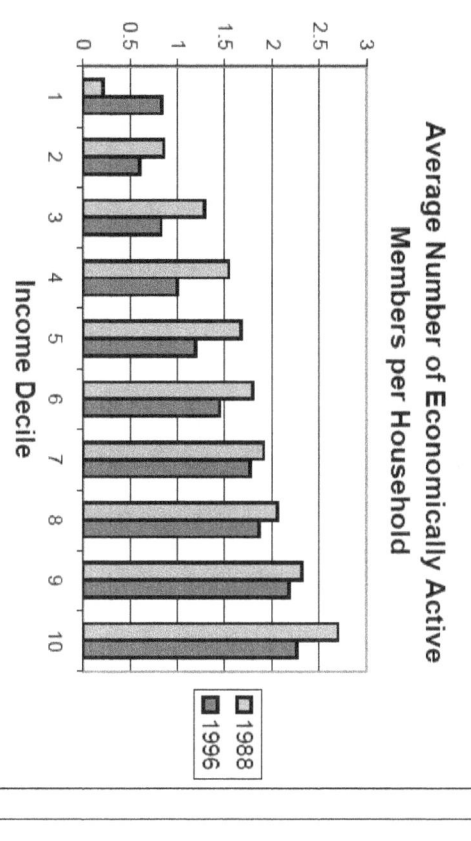

Average Number of Persons per Household

Income Decile

□ 1988
■ 1996

Deciles of persons ranked by equivalent total after tax household income including in-kind -LIS scale

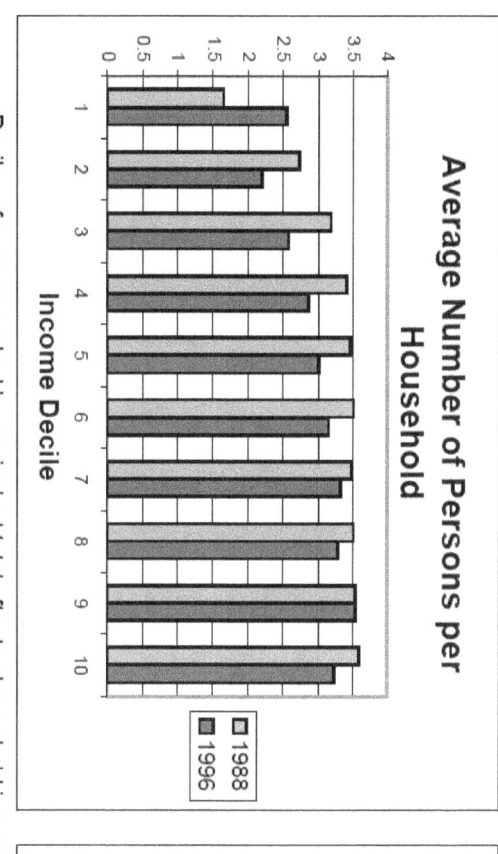

Average Number of Children per Household

Income Decile

□ 1988
■ 1996

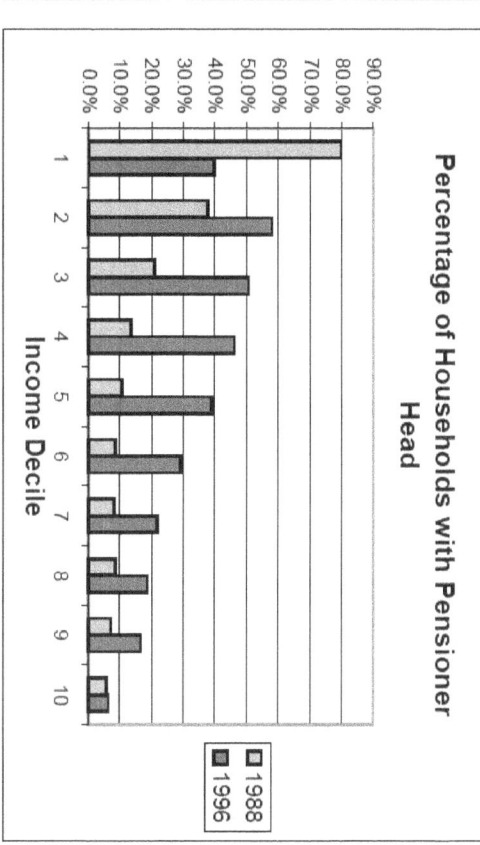

Average Number of Economically Active Members per Household

Income Decile

□ 1988
■ 1996

Deciles of persons ranked by equivalent total after tax household income including in-kind -LIS scale

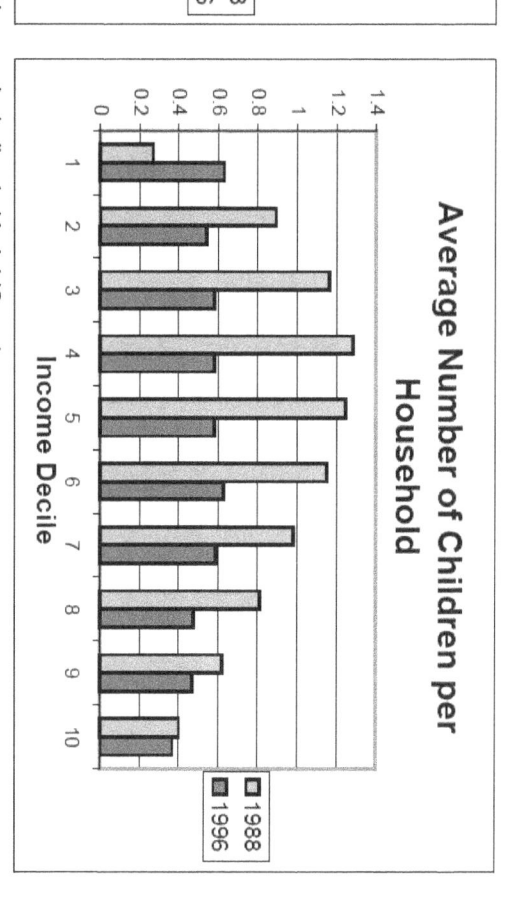

Percentage of Households with Pensioner Head

Income Decile

□ 1988
■ 1996